Evie
WHO FEELS
EVERYTHING

Boom
Pop!
Evie felt things

BIG and small,

sometimes nothing, sometimes all.

A look, a sound, a shift of tone,
could stir a storm she faced alone.

She cried when music
made her ache,

or when her brother
dropped his cake.

She cried when clouds
looked extra gray,
or when a bug got swept
away.

Some kids just shook things
off with ease,
but Evie's heart fell to its
knees.

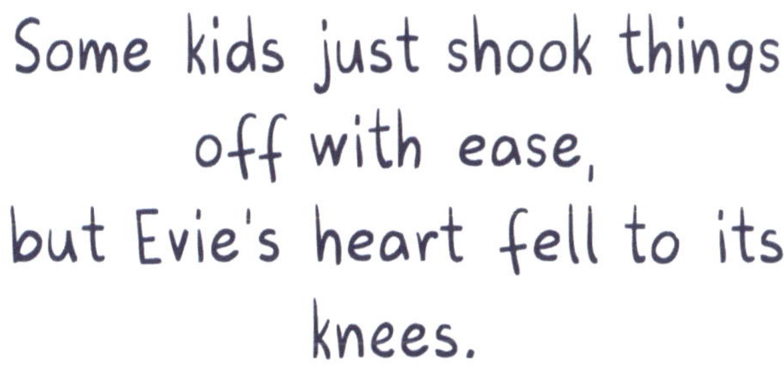

She felt things others didn't see—
like when the wind sighed through a tree.

She'd cry at kindness.

Cry at pain.

Cry when nothing could explain.

And sometimes grown-ups didn't get
why Evie's eyes were always wet.

"Too sensitive", they'd sometimes say.
"Too much to feel. Too much each day."

She tried to hide her tears with pride —
but every time, they still would slide.

She wished that she could just feel less,
Or wear a coat to guard the mess.

But feelings don't work like a switch.
They don't turn off without a glitch.

One morning, tears came fast in class.
A boy called her "delicate as glass".

She ran outside. Her chest felt tight.
She couldn't breathe. It wasn't right.

Then softly came her teacher's voice,
As if she'd given Evie choice:

"It's ok to feel this way.
Your tears don't need to go away."

"There's strength inside a heart like yours,
It opens wide, it deeply pours.
It means you care. It means you see.
It means you feel the world like me".

Evie blinked.
Her breath came slow.
A tiny warmth began to grow.

She noticed someone sitting near,
their mouth was tight. They fought a tear.

She gave her hand, not knowing why.
But somehow, it helped them both not cry.

And from that day, she came to see,

There are other hearts that feel like me.

She laughed and cried, she sang and spun,
Her feelings dancing in the sun.

She didn't try to block the rain,
It watered seeds she'd grow from pain.

And Evie learned, by letting be,
she gave the world a way to see.
That feeling deep is not a flaw,
it's just a heart that's full of awe.

So if you cry and feel things too,
Evie's heart says, "It's okay, I see you."

And if your tears come every day,
Just know they're never wrong to stay.
You feel so much because you care,
And that's a gift you always wear.